The Parachutist

Sundress Publications • Knoxville, TN

Copyright © 2024 by Jose Hernandez
ISBN: 978-1-951979-72-0
Library of Congress: 2024946818
Published by Sundress Publications
www.sundresspublications.com

Managing Editor: Krista Cox
Editorial Assistant: Kanika Lawton
Editorial Interns: Sophia Zhang and Claire Svec

Colophon: This book is set in EB Garamond
Cover Art: "Flying Cactus" by Luisa Azevedo
Cover Design: Kristen Camille Ton
Book Design: Sherrel McLafferty

The Parachutist

Jose Hernandez Diaz

Acknowledgements

Grateful to the editors of the following literary magazines where some of these poems appeared sometimes in different forms.

3:AM Magazine, "Ballad of Kukulkan"
The American Poetry Review, "The Skeleton at the Pier"
The Awl, "The Skeleton and the Guitar"
Bat City Review, "El Mariachi"
Bennington Review, "The Centaur," "The Human Puzzle," and "The Man and the Antlers"
The Best American Nonrequired Reading 2011, "The Border"
Boulevard Magazine, "Decade"
Carve Zine, "Giotto's 'O'"
Chiricú Journal, "The Fighter"
Cincinnati Review, "The Box," "The Fire," and "The Wall"
Colorado Review, "Saludos to the Moon" and "The Tattoo of Montezuma"
The Cortland Review, "Sunflowers in the City"
Cosmonaut Avenue, "The True Poet"
diode poetry journal, "The Cake" and "The Hole"
English Journal (NCTE), "Self-Taught Man"
Frontier Poetry, "Not a Wall"
The Georgia Review, "The Field" and "Making Tamales with Mom on Christmas Eve"
Gigantic Sequins, "The Parrot"
Green Mountains Review, "Aliens," "The Jaguar," and "Kafka's Ghost"
Guesthouse, "The Skeleton at Bat" and "The United States of the Moon"
The Iowa Review, "Taxi to the Beach"
The Journal, "The Guitarist" and "The Man in a Zorro Mask"
Juked, "Deconstruct"
The Missouri Review (Online), "The Dragon and the Coyote"
The Nation, "The Parachutist"
New Delta Review, "The Man and the Leaves"
North American Review, "The Abandoned Shore"
Pangyrus, "The Most Poetic Thing"
Parcel, "Jorge Ramos Is from Guanajuato"

Pleiades, "The Balloon and the Helicopter"
Poet Lore, "The Skeleton and the Book"
Poetry Daily, "Saludos to the Moon"
Poetry Magazine, "Cuauhtémoc Xochipilli," "The Jaguar and the Mango,"
       "Pan Dulce," and "Tecolote"
The Progressive Magazine, "An Ode to Los Jornaleros"
Poetry Northwest, "The Mime and the Old Man" and "The Rose Bush"
Puerto del Sol, "Elegy for a Basketball Court from My Youth"
Rattle, "The Windmill Farm"
Redivider, "Cuates"
Southeast Review, "The Fire Eater"
The South Hampton Review, "El Sombrero" and "Enough"
Sun Dog Lit, "When the Government Wasn't Run by Clowns"
Whale Road Review, "The Skeleton and the Rose"
Zone 3, "When Goya Died, Everything Died"

Some of these poems first appeared in a chapbook "The Fire Eater"
published by Texas Review Press, 2020.

Contents

For my parents, Maria and Esteban Hernandez Vega.

For my siblings. For my cousins, tíos and tías.

For my nephews and nieces.

I.

Jorge Ramos is from Guanajuato

Jorge Ramos is not from Guanajuato.
Jorge Ramos is from Mexico City.

My father insists he is from Guanajuato.
My father is from Guanajuato.

My father takes great pride in saying,
Jorge Ramos is from Guanajuato.

I tell my father; *Jorge Ramos is from Mexico City.*
He is not from Mexico City, my father says,

He is from Cerano, Guanajuato.
Why don't we Google it, I say.

There's no point, my father says,
Jorge Ramos is from Cerano, Guanajuato.

Jorge Ramos is from Guanajuato.

El Mariachi

My dad was a mariachi, but he never made it big.
He played in small shows, Mexican restaurants.
Got paid very little. But he had a loyal following.
He got mail from Chile to San Antonio, Texas.
He once opened for José Alfredo Jiménez in Guanajuato.
My dad once played his guitar on the surface of the moon.
He gave it all up for me. He gave it all up for me.
My dad plays the guitar. My dad plays the guitar.
My dad was a mariachi and fame never meant anything to him.

The Self-Taught Man

My dad never got a chance to go to school as a boy.
He was raised on a rancho where there wasn't much
Opportunity, but to work around the house and the fields.

When he came to the States, he worked in the kitchens,
Learned English words on the spot, and eventually he started taking
ESL classes at night. He learned English little by little,
Ultimately getting to the point where he began to question his instructors,

Non-conformist that he's always been. Now, at 72, I bring
Him to the public library for the first time to get a library card.
He checks out a book about senior health and a religious book.

He spends his time reading in bed when he's not working.
I bring him a green tea and ask what he's reading.
"I'm reading about the foods I need to eat," he says.

Sometimes, I wonder what dad would've been with that work ethic,
And that intelligence, if he'd had a chance in life. Probably a poet,
Professor, like me, I think, or whatever he'd like to be;

Besides, he's already a saint.

The Fighter

My mom was raised on a small rancho in Guanajuato, Mexico.
She went to elementary school for a couple years, but then
She had to stop going to help take care of her siblings.

When she made it to the States she was fascinated by her
New country, but also kept pushing. She started taking ESL classes
At the local library. She always kept an eye out for garage sales

So that my siblings and I could have clothes for school.
As we got older, she started working in fast food restaurants
And hospitals, going to community college for Child Development

At night. She started working as a teacher's aide for a few years
Before eventually getting hired as a preschool teacher.
She held that position for 25 years. My mother never met a fight

She couldn't win. Or she'd at least go down swinging.

The Field
For my mother

As my mom is making handmade tortillas de maíz
to eat with fajitas for lunch, I ask her, "Mom,
do you have any stories from your childhood in México?"
She says yes, as if she's been waiting for me to ask

her that her whole life. Let me tell you.
One time when we were kids, my father told me
and your tío Trini to go with him to the fields—
he had a job for us. Our job was to guard the sowed field

from the quails with makeshift slingshots made from rags.
He also instructed us to yell at the birds, woosha, woosha!
when they approached the dirt in the fields,
to scare them off. So, my father went back home

to sow another small field, by our house.
We were alone for a while, doing the job,
yelping and shooting rocks at the quails
when they darted to the floor to try and dig up the seeds.

But Dad had built a swing for us on a nearby tree,
and told us we could also play on the swing
while we worked, switching back and forth.
So, it wasn't all bad. We did this for a couple of hours,

but then started to wonder where Dad was.
I started to panic and told my younger brother,
who was seven, that I was worried.
Mom had told us a story when we were even younger

of a man who went to the fields to lose his children.
I was sure this was happening to us now.
My brother looked at me with deep fear in his eyes,
and we started crying. After crying for a while

in the bright field, we decided to try and go back home.
It was about an hour away from the house,
but we were going to try, anyway, without any other option.
I told my brother that in the story Mom told us,

about the kids who were abandoned by their father,
they followed orange peels they'd left on the road
along the way and they were able to find home.
I said, we don't have any orange peels to follow right now,

but we're going to find home anyway.
After about twenty minutes of walking, though,
my brother said he was hungry. I told him
to wait by the dirt road, and I went into the bushes

to get a tuna de nopal. As I tore the giant tuna from the nopal,
a sharp thorn thrust into the palm of my hand,
and I threw the tuna to the floor and started crying
and shaking. After a few minutes of drama,

my brother helped me remove the thorn.
It was still bleeding a little, but we had to keep going.
It was actually still daytime, Maybe 2 p.m.,
but it felt like forever since we saw Dad.

We didn't know exactly where we were going,
but we walked and walked, and eventually found home
in the rancho. Dad was surprised and upset to see us
when we walked in the house. "What are you doing here?

Why did you leave the field?" he said. I responded,
crying, "Usted nos fue a perder. Nunca vino.
You left us there to get rid of us." He started laughing, loudly.
"Estan locos! Jajaja. I just left you there for an hour

or two to work and you both panicked.
I was still sowing the field here and was halfway done
with the work. I was going to pick you up after lunch,
I promise," he said. Mom and Dad then gave

us both a hug and comforted us. They told us they would
never leave us. We felt better. We were hungry,
so we ate tacos with frijoles and drank water.
When Mom finishes telling me this story,

back in Southern California, I tell her,
I wrote a poem about the story you just told me, Mom.
Well, technically, you wrote it, I said.

Pan Dulce

My niece calls me from my brother-in-law's phone
While I'm getting ready to wash dishes. I pick up.

She says she needs to talk to her grandfather.
I tell her that her grandfather just went to sleep,

And gave specific instructions not to wake him.
She says to wake him up, she needs to talk to him.

I say OK and hope it's not something bad.
She speaks to her grandfather in English. My dad

Responds to her in "broken" English, but she can't really
Understand him. He gives me back the phone, frustrated.

I ask her what's wrong. She says her school project
Is to ask a grandparent to tell them an uplifting story.

I tell her I'll ask him in Spanish and then call her back
And tell her the story. I tell dad, *Natalia quiere saber*

Un cuento del triunfo; algo de triunfar, I tell him,
About your childhood. He says he doesn't have a story.

I tell him, *like a story when I submitted to a magazine for
Four years, and on the fifth year got in*. He nods his head.

OK, he says. Dad proceeds to tell me about his
Childhood, when he was seven or eight years old.

He says his father taught him how to make pan dulce
From scratch. He says he felt proud about making the bread,

And after they baked it, they sold it in the street.
I tell him that's a perfect story and that pan dulce

Is my favorite. He nods again. Before I call my niece back,
I finish washing the dishes, then rush to my laptop,

To write this poem.

Making Tamales with Mom on Christmas Eve

Mama made miracles every Thanksgiving.
—Tupac Shakur, "Dear Mama"

I can write odes all day to Mom's tortillas,
frijoles, quesadillas, tostadas, sopas,
chiles, salsas, enchiladas, tacos, banana nut bread,
chorizo con huevo, flautas; the list goes on.

If Mom wasn't working or at church, she was in the kitchen:
Hustling to make a meal out of a 99-cent-store budget.
Sure, it wasn't all that healthy, but it was tasty and filling,
and damn it was consistent. We were probably

spoiled as kids. Not in the sense that we had a lot,
but Mom made the illusion that we had more than enough;
the way she stretched things. Only buying on sale.
Going to garage sales. Swap meets. Food-giveaways.

I will build a statue in her honor. This Christmas,
for the first time, I rolled up my sleeves,
an adult now, and helped Mom make the tamales.
I can tell she felt a little uncomfortable at first,

as if I might mess it up. Lol. But we eventually had fun with it.
No, the tamales didn't turn out as good as we wanted.
But we had fun, and we will always have that memory.
Thank you, Mom, for taking care of me

when I couldn't take care of myself;
And even when I could. I probably didn't deserve it,
but you never let me down.

Tecolote

The Mexican word for owl is tecolote, from the Nahuatl: tecolotl.
I think it sounds beautiful in both languages: both of my origins.

My favorite bird is the tecolote. The way it sits in the tree:
Wise insomniac, alone. Only company is rain. At night, it comes alive:

A little moon. A myth. A continent of leaves. At midnight: the tecolote
Transforms into a jaguar, into a python, into a dragon.

When I was younger, my mom used to tell me I was like
A tecolote because I would stay up late to watch Letterman or

Conan O'Brien. Then, as a teenager, I was a tecolote because I would
Go out late with friends and party. Now, at thirty-five, I'm getting

A tattoo of a tecolote on my forearm. Reminder of my childhood,
My ancestry, the night. Gracias, tecolote: protector of the moon and sky.

The True Poet

My abuelo was the true poet:
The way he tilled the land with his hands,
Beneath the sun; he seemed to touch the sky

With his hoe. My abuelo was the true poet:
The way he joked with his mule as they rode,
The two of them alone with the dawn;

He seemed to reach the moon with his laugh.
My abuelo was the true poet: the way
He smoked his cigarette on the porch like a train

In the wind; he seemed to graze the trees
With his breath. My abuelo was the true poet:
The way he wrote the earth with his poems;

He could not use a pen with his hands.

Cuates

When my twin brother tells me stories about
His troubled youth: running with gangs, drugs, etc.

I think how lucky he is, and I am, and the family is
That nothing worse happened to him. I know he's

Actually a good guy, even though he ran with wolves.
I think he was always looking for companionship.

He found it in fellow bald-headed misfits: latchkey kids
Who lived in low-rent apartments in middle-class suburbs.

Maybe I was a bad twin brother. I had sports. I had friends.
I know I don't owe him an apology, though: he'd just laugh it off.

Besides, we've become closer now that we're in our thirties.
Watch sports together. Go to the same libraries. Have lunch together.

No point in dwelling on the past. Adelante. Siempre adelante.
But I do find it ironic that I can never remember the distinction

Between the Spanish words for identical and fraternal twins.
Let me look it up: gemelos means identical twins; same egg.

Cuates means fraternal twins; different egg, like us.

II.

The Border

They have built a border:
At the dinner table, when they want their fruits and vegetables—
Between sweaty fields and their inherent privilege.

They have built a border:
At the car wash, when they want their luxury vehicles polished—
Spotless, sir—
Between breaking backs and their abundant vanity.

They have built a border:
Behind the picket fence, when they want their gardens groomed—
A little less roses, sir—
Between the roots of honest labor and blooming decadence.

They have built a border:
At the drive-thru window, when they want fast food—
Between a minimum wage and an artificial convenience.

They have built a border:
In their industry, when they want their factories fine-tuned—
Between diligence and mechanized indifference.

They have built a border:
At the curb of Home Depot, when they want jornaleros—
Between cheap labor and the structures of discrimination.

An Ode to Los Jornaleros

They rise at dawn
And cross themselves
La Virgen knows
She knows it well

They sit and wait
On crooked curbs
For dirty work
They sit and wait

And when work comes
Trucks pick them up
They rush and shout
Like sheltered dogs

The jobs they get
Are hard and cheap
They twist and sweat
They bend and bleed

They push and mow
For daily bread
They stack and build
For milk and meat

Behind the wall
They send the cash
To México
They send it all

The laws that stand
Cause them to fall
To hide and squirm
This country's hell

Before they sleep
They cross themselves
La Virgen knows
She knows it well

Deconstruct

I'm Chicano. I used to want to write graffiti.
Socially-conscious graffiti. I didn't want to be fined,
Or go to jail. The only graffiti I had the courage to write
Was the word, '*deconstruct*,' in the restroom at Wheeler Hall.
I wrote it because I was pretentious. Because I was rebellious.
Because I thought it would sound important and artistic.
Only it was barely legible. I grew up writing on computers.
Or maybe I just naturally have bad penmanship.
I don't think '*deconstruct*' has mass appeal. I wanted it
To not have appeal. But some appeal. Choice appeal.
The color I chose, burgundy.

Giotto's "O"

I remember the first time I heard
The story of Giotto's "O." How he

Was sought after by the Pope, along
With other pre-renaissance painters,

To paint several paintings on commission
For Saint Peter's Basilica in the Vatican,

And when the Pope's men came to
Giotto's studio in Florence and asked

For a painting sample to bring back to Rome,
Giotto dipped his brush in paint and

Painted a simple "O." That's it. Nothing more.
It was enough for the Pope to see his talent.

It was enough to start a renaissance.
So, when I think of this story and how it

Led me to study more paintings and then
More poetry, when I was lost after undergrad,

I feel blessed in a way. Not in a religious way,
Necessarily, but just lucky to have the opportunity

To study art, despite the world continuing to tell me
It's a waste of time. A waste of a life.

Picasso's Skull

You're far away, in Southern France,
In the Château de Vauvenargues, resting in peace.

I'm here in a library in Southeast L.A.,
Reading about your various moods.

I think of the cool air in autumn in Málaga,
When you were young, throwing purple leaves

In your direction. It must've been
Something to see you draw your first cube

On your living room couch.
I remember as a young Latinx man,

Wishing my last name was Picasso.
Or admiring how you and Neruda made Pablo—

An otherwise common, boring name—
Something to be proud of.

I once drew you on a skateboard
and called it "The Path."

If you had been raised in SELA
Would you have been a famous graffiti artist

Like the Latinx youth who speak Spanish here?
The cube, the blue, the rose, the bullfighter,

The Christ, the depth, the death, the silence.
You: Master of it all. All of us:

Your grateful offspring.

Enough

You will never be enough.
Not Chicano enough.
Not Pocho enough.
Not Mexican enough.
Not Latinx enough.
Not American enough.
Not Californian enough.
Not Southern Californian enough.
Not L.A. County enough.
Not Orange County enough.
Not enough of a whole entity.
Not enough of a clear sky.
Not enough of a bottle of tequila.
Not enough of a slice of apple pie.
But you are everything and nothing—
All at once.
You are a modern Mariachi
on a tangled road:
be vigilant. Exist.

Saludos to the Moon

Sometimes I wish my Spanish were better,
Like to the point where I could speak it without

Having to think about it. I can get by, trust me,
But it's broken. Like that trendy restaurant downtown:

Broken Spanish. It would be nice to write poems in Spanish
Or even a mix of both languages. But my instinct, it seems,

Is to lean on the language I have mastered. For now, at least,
I can throw in a word, here and there, like tesoro.

Language es un tesoro. The moon, tesoro. Leaves: tesoro.
My computer always marks Spanish words as misspelled.

I want to say, todo bien. Hasta la ultima palabra.
In my neighborhood or barrio, it is mostly Mexican or

Mexican-American. Five gangs in the neighborhood.
I've never had a problem. There are also many hard-working

Blue-collar factory workers. No pretention. Grit. Muchas ganas.
Many have served or serve in the military, and even though

I'm very liberal, I don't judge them because honestly
If I hadn't found writing in high school, I probably

Would've served, too, without many other options.
I never know how to end a poem, especially a poem

That I didn't expect to write; but I will go back to some more
Spanish words: Adiós. Adiós to the sun and the skyline,

Tonight. Saludos. Saludos to the moon with her accent so bright.

Elegy for a Basketball Court from My Youth

When I was a boy, twenty, thirty years ago,
I wanted to be a professional basketball player.

I was pretty good, I played with the neighborhood kids
From the apartments, they were all older than me,

But I had a street-style of play, as opposed to the gym style
Which is prominent in high schools, even to this day.

I was good at throwing behind-the-back passes
And dribbling behind my back, but I lacked basic

Fundamentals like dribbling well with the left hand, or having
A consistent outside shot, which for a point-guard is crucial.

I did have good defense. I could guard guys twice my size
When they would post me up. I always led the game in steals.

But, when I eventually made it to high school, the coach
Told me to focus on football, where I was a starter.

The last time I shot the basketball at my neighborhood park,
With my friends, was the day before my brothers got

Into a gang rumble at the same park. Luckily, everyone survived,
But I'm told there were multiple weapons. I was the one who'd called

The police. After football practice, when my friend's mom
Picked us up, I told her the rumor was my brothers

And their friends were going to rumble, with weapons,
At the park behind our apartments. So, I called the police.

Long story short, we drove by the park, later, to check it out,
My friend's step-dad was a former convict who had ran

With gangs in his younger days, he told us not to worry.
Well, when we finally got there, all we found was our family car:

Busted up and tagged over, windows shattered. I never went back
To that park anymore. It wasn't safe, anymore. Even if one day

It would be safe again, like today, for example. It's already too late.
The damage is done. Basketball, but a mere memory of youth.

The Most Poetic Thing

At 6 a.m., I read Lorca's *Poema del Cante Jondo*. I take a photo
Of "La Lola" in the sunlight and post it on Facebook and Instagram.

The talented poet Dara Wier likes it. That makes my day.
Then, I submit poems to a literary magazine and prepare

My submissions for August 1st, when a few more journals open.
Also, I edit a prose poem about a dragon and a horse rider.

In the evening, when I'm finishing up some work on the computer
At the local library, an O.G. from the neighborhood with gang tattoos

Covering his body and face walks in the library with his daughters
And helps them look for books. They tell him the names of the books,

And he says "Let's look for them alphabetically." I can't help but smile,
As one of the toughest guys in the barrio is in the children's section

Of the library looking for books with his kids. Much respect, though,
I keep thinking: that's the most poetic thing I've seen all day.

Ballad of Kukulkan

sacred feathered snake
        jaguar jade and purple sun
            sacred feathered snake

            jaguar jade and purple sun
        thirteen rabbit rise
eagle drum and orange moon

thirteen rabbit rise
        eagle drum and orange moon
            shadows on the lake

            floating gardens feathers bloom
        shadows on the lake
floating gardens feathers bloom

III.

"We have to laugh. Because laughter, we already know, is the first evidence of freedom."
—Rosario Castellanos,
A Rosario Castellanos Reader

The Cake

A man in a Pink Floyd shirt jumped over a sycamore tree.
He did not jump over a sycamore tree.

He flew over a castle. He did not fly over a castle.
He swam in a volcano. He did not swim in a volcano.

He drove to the circus. He did not drive to the circus.
He laughed at a grizzly bear. He did not laugh at a grizzly bear.

He juggled a dagger. He did not juggle a dagger.
He ate all the cake. He did not eat all the cake.

Yes. Yes, he did.

The Astronaut

A man in a Pink Floyd shirt woke up on his living room couch. There was a party going on in the house. The man in the Pink Floyd shirt didn't recognize anyone at the party. He wasn't drunk. He tapped a man in a green sweater's shoulder, "Hello, who are you?" he asked. "I'm Gary," he said. "Yes, but what are you all doing here?" the man in the Pink Floyd shirt asked. "We are celebrating your graduation from astronaut training, of course," the man in the green sweater said. "Of course," the man in a Pink Floyd shirt said. He didn't actually recall being an astronaut. In fact, he hated math and science. Was more of an arts and crafts guy. Besides, he had an incredible fear of heights. The next thing he knew, the guests were handing out glasses for champagne and a toast. They started chanting, "Speech! Speech!"

The man in a Pink Floyd shirt grabbed a glass of champagne and stood in front of the eager crowd. He raised his glass, cleared his throat, and then spoke, "I'd like to thank you all for coming tonight. I'm honored by your presence. I've wanted to be an astronaut since I was a little boy growing up in the mountains of Arizona. I used to dream about existence beyond the clouds. Now my dreams are coming true. Reach for the stars, friends. Never let fear defeat you. Cheers to space! Cheers to all of you!" he said. The crowd erupted in cheer and they clinked their glasses together. They had long conversations until after midnight when they began to disperse. After everyone was gone, the man in a Pink Floyd shirt went to sleep and dreamt about another world's dawn. Another galaxy, even.

The Balloon and the Helicopter

A man in a Pink Floyd shirt sat by a window. He saw a balloon rise and rise. The balloon crashed into a helicopter. The helicopter sliced the balloon into countless pieces. The man in a Pink Floyd shirt laughed and laughed. It began to rain. The man in a Pink Floyd shirt pulled a book from the shelf. The book was called, *The Balloon and the Helicopter*. He opened the book, closed it, and went to the kitchen to make coffee. He couldn't find coffee, so he decided to go to the store. When he opened the door, he found hundreds if not thousands of pieces of balloon on the front porch. The man in a Pink Floyd shirt laughed and laughed. *What a day*, he said to himself. *What a day?* He returned to the window and gazed away, looking for another balloon. Then the man in a Pink Floyd shirt thought of coffee again and returned to the kitchen. *Oh yes,* he said. *I need to go to the store for coffee. What a day*, the man in a Pink Floyd shirt said. *What a day?*

The Hole

A man in a Pink Floyd shirt dug a giant hole in his backyard. Someone had told him to go to hell earlier that day. Assuming hell to be beneath the soil, the man in a Pink Floyd shirt picked up a shovel, and got to work. The person who told him to go to hell was a professional juggler. He juggled axes, bowling pins, and soccer balls. The man in a Pink Floyd shirt had accidentally bumped into him causing him to drop his soccer balls. That's when he told him to go to hell. The man in a Pink Floyd shirt dug and dug. He told himself when he got to hell, he would fistfight Lucifer. He didn't much like his chances against Lucifer, but he thought it a noble endeavor. Finally, at midnight, the man in a Pink Floyd shirt dropped his shovel from fatigue, and fell asleep inside the hole. When he woke up the next day, he no longer wanted to dig a hole to hell. He just wanted black coffee. Black coffee with toast and eggs. *Bon appétit, man in a Pink Floyd shirt.*

When the Government Wasn't Run by Clowns

A man in a Pink Floyd shirt went to the library downtown. He checked out a book about the government. He was trying to figure it all out. The government was run by men from the planet Jupiter. Apparently, one must be 5.88 trillion years old to run for office. The head of the government is a clown with an axe. Every now and then he juggles the axe when he's drunk on his own power. The clown with the axe is running for reelection. He holds rallies and parades with mastodons, tarantulas, and puppets. The man in a Pink Floyd shirt puts the book down in horror. He drinks his coffee. He writes a poem on the back of his hand. It's about the government, yes, but also hope. It's called "When the Government Wasn't Run by Clowns."

When Goya Died, Everything Died

A man in a Pink Floyd shirt rode the subway to the city. He listened to a woman play the violin on the train as it rumbled over the crooked streets. The man in a Pink Floyd shirt had a pocket full of leaves. Red leaves. Yellow leaves. Brown leaves. It was autumn, yes, but it was also his birthday month. He was born on October 31st: Halloween. Every year he dressed up as David Gilmour and put on a show for his neighborhood. He has quite the voice and talent. He's played the guitar since the age of five.

When the train arrived to the field of dandelions, the man in a Pink Floyd shirt got off and sat on a bench. He painted a picture of the field of dandelions. He titled it "When Goya Died, Everything Died." He sold the painting for $111,000.00. He used the money to open up a marijuana dispensary in his hometown, by the ocean. He doesn't smoke. He's just an acute businessman.

The Box

A man in a Pink Floyd shirt was stuck in a box. It was a cardboard box. He started punching at the box. Eventually, it gave in. When he jumped out of the box he realized he was being shipped to England. The man in a Pink Floyd shirt had never been to England, even though he majored in English Literature in undergrad. The man began to realize he could finally see some of the sites from the poems he'd read: Tintern Abbey, Big Ben, River Thames, etc., so he got back into the box. He arrived in England in 7-10 business days. He walked in the streets. He admired the fog. He listened to the accents. He wrote poems about his visit. On his last day in England, he had a pint of ale and watched a soccer match. At sunset, he got back into the box and returned to California. He loved the box. He loved his life.

The United States of the Moon

A man in a Pink Floyd shirt fell asleep on a rocking chair on the moon. He had a dream about the government. The government gave him a salary of $235,000 per year because he was a famous astronaut. He was building a civilization on the moon. The nation was going to be called The United States of the Moon. His chair was still rocking as he slept. Fifteen of his fellow astronauts had come with him to start a civilization on the moon. They were from various Earth countries, including, Mexico, Japan, and Australia. None of the astronauts were very good at poker. One of them was a saint. The rest were common astronauts.

Then a moonquake happened. The man in a Pink Floyd shirt jumped out of his rocking chair. He bounced around the moon. It shook for an hour. When it was over, all that survived was the space ship and the man in a Pink Floyd shirt. He boarded the space ship with tears in his eyes. He flew toward Earth, wounded, but not defeated.

The Skeleton at Bat

A man in a Pink Floyd shirt plucked an azalea from a garden. It was the beginning of spring. The sun was shining, nicely. He thought about how happy he was he hadn't smoked a cigarette in three weeks. He took a deep breath. He drank some water. He decided to take the azalea to his girlfriend. She said, "Thank you for the beautiful flower!" They embraced. Then he went home and painted for three hours. He drank coffee. But his paintings were not flowery at all. They were rather dark. But it brought him peace. He fell asleep after he painted a skeleton smoking a cigarette beneath the moonlight.

When the man in a Pink Floyd shirt woke up the next day, he rode his longboard to the Venice Boardwalk. He sold his painting for $150. He considered it a successful day. He went home and ate and then watched the Dodger game. Later, when he finished watching the game, he decided to paint a skeleton with a Dodgers jersey, swinging a bat at Dodger Stadium under the lights. He called it, "The Skeleton at Bat." The next day he sold it for another $150. It was turning into a very productive week, indeed. He loved spring. And skeletons. And the moon. And the Dodgers.

The Guitarist

A man in a Pink Floyd shirt threw a football toward the top of a skyscraper in Downtown Los Angeles. He was trying to prove a point to his girlfriend. He told her he could throw a football as high as a skyscraper. The girlfriend thought he was crazy but followed him downtown anyway. The man in a Pink Floyd shirt was just trying to impress her. He thought she was the type who would be impressed by a strong arm. After his failed throw, the girlfriend explained to him, *just be yourself.* Then they lived happily ever after. That is, until he lost his job at the rocking chair factory. He worked hard with his hands, building rocking chairs. He wasn't exactly proud of his work, but work is work. The man in a Pink Floyd shirt was fired because he refused to put on his uniform one day. "Take off that Pink Floyd shirt!" his boss said. "I refuse!" the man in a Pink Floyd shirt said. He was fired right around the holidays. Then his girlfriend broke up with him. He now plays a mean guitar. *Rest in peace, man in a Pink Floyd shirt.*

IV.

The Centaur

I was ordered to go to hell after I died. When I arrived, I found a large centaur with a shotgun guarding the entrance. "I've been ordered to go to hell," I said. "Yes, license, please," the centaur said. "What license?" I said, "I'm naked." "After you died, didn't you see a Mr. Jay Williamson at registration?" the centaur asked. "Yes, he ordered me to come here." "Didn't he give you an ID card and chewing gum?" he said. "No, just chewing gum." "Well, you'll have to go back and get proper identification. There isn't much we can do without that license," he said. "This is very inconvenient, and, frankly, unprofessional," I said. "Next in line!" the centaur said.

The Parrot

It had been raining so I was anxious to get back to the apartment. When I arrived I found a large parrot sitting at my writing desk. It was blue and orange with yellow triangular marks. "Hello," I say. "Hello, Mr. Gonzalez." "I beg your pardon," I say. "Good evening, Mr. Gonzalez," it repeats. "I'm not a Gonzalez. I'm a Hollis-Ordóñez," I say. "No, you're Mr. Gonzalez," it says. "You're a star first baseman for the Los Angeles Dodgers." "I'm a banker!" I say. "You're clutch in late innings, and your Spanish is fluent. You're an outstanding tipper. But not a rico-suave. You've contributed to charitable organizations without taking credit." "I'm a slugger and a captain," I agree, "I'm on deck and I'm fearless."

The Jaguar

As I enter the garage to lift weights, I hear a vicious roar. To my surprise,
I find a turquoise jaguar sitting on the washer. I drop my water bottle and
run back to the kitchen. I retrieve a birthday cake from the fridge and throw
it to the jaguar. It's not the jaguar's birthday, but it's hungry nonetheless.
When the jaguar finishes the cake, I give it the requisite gifts. Five gifts in
total, none more appreciated than a sling shot. The jaguar roars for joy,
revealing it didn't have a happy childhood. As a result of the gifts and cake,
the jaguar and I build a strong bond that I cherish for many years. When the
jaguar dies of old age, three heads of state and four archbishops attend the
somber funeral. The jaguar had lived humbly. It lived fully.

The Human Puzzle

I woke up and discovered I was a human jigsaw puzzle. My foot was one piece. My head was two pieces. My torso was divided into three peculiar pieces. When I tried to get up to make coffee, I could only move in slow motion. The puzzle pieces were various shades of blue: Cambridge, cerulean, Columbia. I didn't know what to do, so I called the police. "I've transformed into a giant puzzle!" I shouted. "You're confused and puzzled?" she asked. "No, I've turned into a giant jigsaw puzzle!" I continued. "Okay, remain calm, sir, we'll send someone over," she said. I hung up and lay on the floor: scattered. *I'm puzzled*, I thought to myself; *the world is a giant puzzle.*

The Windmill Farm

I was drawing a windmill onto the fog in the mirror after a shower, when I thought, *Why am I drawing a windmill onto the fog in the mirror?* Then I answered, *I'm drawing a windmill because it is a metaphor for rain.* Next, I wiped the windmill off the mirror with my towel, and got ready for work. I work at a windmill farm 45 miles east of Los Angeles. The job consists mostly of staring at windmills. Mondays we meditate under the windmills, the company brings in a yogi with a PhD in Philosophy. Tuesdays are Texas hold 'em Tuesdays. Wednesdays we stare at the windmills with absolute fear. Thursdays we check for mechanical failures and other duties as necessary. Fridays, Fridays we wipe the windmill blades clean of flies and mosquito guts. Then on weekends I watch boxing and long for the swooshing sounds of the windmill farm. Weekends are tough, but it's only two days.

The Parachutist

I was smoking a cigarette in the backyard after a long day at work, when a man in a parachute fell from the sky, right into the lilac bushes. I tossed the cigarette and ran up to him. "Are you okay?" I said. "I'm fine, just happy to get away from the enemy," he said. "The enemy? What enemy?" I said. "The enemy otherwise known as the mundane," he said. "That's peculiar," I said. "Be that as it may, the mundane has waged merciless war on me and millions of my fellow Americans for years," he said. "Would you like some water or lemonade? You've been through a lot," I said. "No, but do you happen to have a helicopter? I'd like to make another jump," he said. "Another random jump to nowhere? What good will that do?" I said. "It will do a lot of good. So much good, that I will no longer feel absolute pain," he said. "Surely there are other ways to deal with pain," I said. "Do you have some whiskey and cola?" the man said. "I've got a bottle or two," I said. "New plan," he said, "we drink the whiskey and cola and play darts on that maple tree." "Great idea!" I said, rushing for the drinks. I was beginning to understand his war against the mundane.

The Man in a Zorro Mask

I fell down the stairs in my house. I was running away from a storm. The storm was upstairs. It wasn't winter, but it was stormy nonetheless. I got up from the floor and sprinted out the door. I didn't know where I was going, but I just wanted to get away from the storm. All the sudden I saw a water well and immediately stopped. It looked like it was from the 18th century. I looked down the empty well and saw a man in a Zorro mask painting a portrait. The portrait was of an average bucolic scene in nature. I called down to the man in a Zorro mask, "Hello! Do you need help?!" "No, I'm fine, thank you! Just painting a portrait of nature," he said. "Why do you paint nature?" I asked. "Because it's all that I need," he said. "Then why not come up here away from your isolation and paint in nature?" I said. "No, it works better down here," he said. "When I deprive myself of nature, it fuels the art." "Makes sense," I said, "be well, man in a Zorro mask!"

Aliens

I wanted to dream about deep space, so I Googled "*aliens*" and stared at photos of them until bed time. None of the photos were of actual aliens, of course, but I wanted to have artificial dreams anyway. Just before I fell asleep, I played Eric Dolphy on Spotify, figuring it was out there and probably appealed to aliens. I began to dream. My dreams had nothing to do with aliens. I was a boy again. I was playing basketball at the park by my childhood home. I did spin move after spin move and threw behind-the-back passes to my friends. I didn't miss a single three-point shot. When I woke there were tears running down my cheeks. I turned the music off and took a cold shower. I made the coffee extra strong and headed off to work.

Kafka's Ghost

I had a dream I was Kafka's ghost. I held a dahlia in my hand. I painted
the walls of the room with the flower. No one else was there. I fell asleep.
When I woke I heard a horse outside the door. I opened the door and rode
to the beach. I fell asleep on the sand. I had a dream I wrote a novel. When
I woke I saw a ship approaching shore. I filled my pockets with seashells. A
lone skeleton captain steered the ship. I scoured my blade and boarded. We
headed west.

V.

El Sombrero

A man fell into the ocean. The water was blue and green. It was the beginning of winter. Luckily, he wore a giant sombrero. He jumped into the sombrero and floated along the shore. The inside of the sombrero was warm and leathered. The clouds spelled out the word: ocean.

Inevitably, the sombrero landed ashore, and the man stepped onto the cool sand. As the moon rose, he sang a ranchera; he was very happy. He walked home beneath the moonlight but left the sombrero behind. It was ruined from the water, but it had saved his life.

The Man and the Antlers

A man picked wild berries in the forest, ate them, and suddenly grew antlers. He was shocked. He ran around in circles, *Why? Why?* Then he saw a small creek. He looked into the water; he saw his antlers in the reflection, strong and sharp. *Why me?* He said. *Why me?* Then a bear approached him. He was startled for a moment, but then charged at the bear with force.

The Man and the Leaves

A man chased leaves down an urban street. The leaves moved fast. He ran and ran. A young boy stopped him, "Sir, why are you chasing leaves?" "I'm a starving artist, I haven't eaten in days!" the man said. "Have some oatmeal cookies," the boy said. "I only eat leaves!" the man said, running down the street. "I only eat leaves!"

Taxi to the Beach

A man hailed a taxi outside of his apartment. He was going to the beach. Suddenly, his fedora caught on fire from his cigarette. He fanned it outside the taxi window. Then his phone rang. It was the President of Mars. "Mr. Lopez, we need your vote next week. Can we count on you?" the President asked. "My hat is on fire!" Mr. Lopez shouted. "I'm sorry to hear that, Mr. Lopez, we'll send you a new one," the President of Mars said. "Thanks, Mr. President, but I can't vote for you," Mr. Lopez said. "Then you don't get a hat. That's how it works. Goodbye!" the President said. Mr. Lopez hung-up and tossed the flaming fedora out of the window. "To the beach!" he shouted.

The Fire

A man woke up in a burning building. He ran to the front door. It was jammed. Then he threw a chair through the window. It shattered and glass fell everywhere. He was careful as he climbed out of the window. It was a three-story building. A preacher was down at the bottom, waiting to catch him. He jumped into the preacher's arms. On impact, they both transformed into pigeons. They flew away from the fire. Far away from the fire.

The Fire Eater

A fire eater performed his tricks on Hollywood Blvd by the entrance to the 101 Freeway. It was autumn. Just as he was about to inhale the bright flame, however, he slipped on a leaf and fell into the street. A motorcycle swerved out of the way and barely missed him. The fire eater quickly got up and jumped back onto the curb. He counted his lucky stars. One star. Two stars. Three stars. But there was no reason to go on. At least he felt that way at the moment. His family of circus performers had abandoned him. He would have to make it on his own. Perhaps he could go back to school? Who was he kidding? Eating fire was his only skill. It wasn't much of a marketable skill, either. Maybe he could make it on *America's Got Talent*? Or get hired in a Vegas show? These were his hopes and dreams. But were they merely pipe dreams? For now, at least, he would have to be content with eating fire on Hollywood Blvd by the 101 Freeway. Maybe someone important would discover him there, tomorrow. Maybe the flame would no longer scar his autumnal heart.

Sunflowers in the City

A man fell asleep on the subway. He woke up in another city. When he got off the train, it began to rain sunflowers. It was the middle of winter. He lit a cigarette and walked to a park. He sat on a graffitied bench and wrote a poem. The poem was about sunflowers, winter, and the city. He went to the library and submitted the poem to various literary magazines. He titled it, 'Sunflowers in the City.'

The Rose Bush

A man plucked an orange rose from a bush, smelled it, and then burst into flames. The flames eventually died out. Ash. Later, the man's daughter came looking for him. All she found were scattered ashes. The girl then walked up to the bush, picked a blue rose, and smelled it. She quickly turned into water and splashed to the floor. She washed away the ash.

The Mime and the Old Man

A mime fell to the floor and pretended he was dead. A young couple walked by. They stared and pointed but continued on their way. Then a butcher walked by. He tugged on the mime's sleeve. After no response, he too continued on his way. Then an old man walked by. He clapped his hands beside the mime's ear. No response. Then he shouted into his ear. Nothing. Finally, the old man lay on the floor, with the mime, and pretended he was dead.

The Dragon and the Coyote

A man looked into a mirror, but he didn't recognize himself. Instead, he saw a dragon and a coyote engaged in a game of chess. The dragon moved first: middle pawn, two spaces. Then the coyote parroted the move. They stared into each other's eyes. Neither budged.

After three hours, they called it a draw. The dragon flapped its scarlet wings, and flew toward a nearby mountain. The coyote began to howl a lullaby. When the man eventually stopped looking into the mirror, he realized he's the dragon. And he's the coyote. It's always been that way.

The Abandoned Shore

A man woke up on an abandoned shore. He had no idea where he was.
There weren't any people around, only seagulls, sand, and ocean. He picked
up a sand dollar and threw it into the ocean. Then he took off his shirt and
jumped in the water. It was very cold, but it didn't bother him.

Then he saw a ship on the horizon. It had a pirate-skull flag and cannons.
The man quickly exited the water and put on his clothes. He ran as fast as
possible, away from the beach. When he finally stopped running, he was
in the middle of a large city. He was elated to hear the sounds of traffic.
Immediately, he fell asleep at a bus stop, in the middle of the city.

Decade

It was the last day of the decade. He had grown from a seed to a forest. His eyes were no longer yellow. He had a beard of thorn roses. His arms were tattooed with lines from Shakespeare's sonnets. Sure, it was over, but nothing would be forgotten.

The decade had hardened his skull. It was inevitable. Graffiti in the mind. His breastplate was made of aluminum. A violin played before midnight. He was awake, finally. No longer did he roam.

The Wall

A man in a Chicano Batman shirt punched a wall. It was a big wall built by a small man. The man in a Chicano Batman shirt didn't have gloves on as he punched the wall. His fists were like bronze statues. He gave the wall a couple jabs. He gave the wall a right cross. An uppercut. He stepped back and sized up his opponent. Nothing but hate and greed. He swung one last power punch and the wall fell down like a glass house. The wall fell down. Fell down. The wall. The.

Not a Wall

A man ran into a wall. It was not an ordinary wall, actually. It was a cowardly wall. The man wrote a poem on the wall:

Dear wall, you are not a wall at all. You are more like a corpse. A rotting flower, even. You are not a wall at all, in fact, you are as transparent as a drunken poker player. You are not a wall, no, you are actually a mirror: I see my aged brown face, my grey hairs, in your expensive bricks. You are not a wall, but an axe: chopping away limbs and dreams and freedom for all.

VI.

The Skeleton and the Book

A skeleton sat by a lake and read a book. The book was about the origins of the Land of Skeletons. The Land of Skeletons was founded six hundred years ago. The skeletons rose from the grave and demanded their freedom. Long had they waited in the cold earth. The skeletons fought many dragons in order to gain their freedom. Many rode valiant horses to fight their enemy.

When the war was over, the skeletons raised their revered flag: a skeleton and a sword. They began to build a civilization of skeletons. They elected officials. They danced in nightclubs. They surfed in the ocean. War never returned to the Land of Skeletons. They lived in peace with the crows, mountain goats, and the redwoods alike. The Land of the Skeletons is our home.

The Skeleton at the Pier

A skeleton walked on a pier holding a balloon. It was a mild Sunday, 75 degrees. The balloon had a drawing of a shark on a surfboard. The skeleton sat down on a bench and stared at the waves. Plenty of seagulls flew overhead. Some seagulls landed on the pier looking for food. The skeleton smoked a cigarette. Then it walked to the edge of the pier just as the sun was setting. The skeleton took a photo of the sunset and posted it on Instagram. It loved living on the west coast. When it started to get dark, the skeleton headed back home on a black bicycle. It tied the balloon onto the bike frame as it rode in the moonlight.

The Skeleton and the Rose

A skeleton smelled a red rose in a public garden. It was late summer. He listened to Childish Gambino on his cell phone as he sat in the garden. The skeleton began to draw with the rose because it was also a pen. The skeleton drew a knight slaying a dragon at sunset on a Southern California coast. When the skeleton finished the drawing, he gave it to a lady skeleton who was sitting by a fountain of koi fish. The lady skeleton received the drawing and graciously thanked him. It began to rain. The skeleton waved the rose in the air and it turned into an umbrella. The umbrella also had an illustration of a knight slaying a dragon. The skeleton carefully covered the lady skeleton with the umbrella and they walked to a coffee shop.

The Skeleton and the Guitar

A skeleton played an acoustic guitar by a lake. It sang folk songs and patriotic songs. People passed by and placed coins and bills inside the skeleton's hat. Koi fish swam in the lake beside the skeleton. At sunset, the skeleton played one final song. It was written by the skeleton. It was called "The Skeleton and the Guitar." The crowd cheered at the end of the song. As the cheers faded, the skeleton collected its belongings, and rode its horse home to the edge of the city.

Cuauhtémoc Xochipilli

A jaguar sat in a tree. It was mid-summer. The sun was shining fiercely. The jaguar was a golden color with plenty of brown spots. Then the ghost of Emiliano Zapata walked by. He was in full uniform, with rifle and sword, but in black-and-white. He looked like a cloud.

The jaguar leapt from the tree and walked up to Zapata's ghost. The jaguar genuflected in General Zapata's direction. Zapata pulled out his sword and knighted the jaguar. "From this day forward, this noble jaguar will be called Cuauhtémoc Xochipilli," he said. The sun faded and set. It began to rain.

The Jaguar and the Mango

A mango fell from a tree into a jaguar's paws. It was late-summer. The jaguar devoured the fruit and ran into the ocean. The ocean was turquoise like the August sky. The jaguar swam underwater for a few minutes. It smiled beneath the waves.

Later, clouds began to form. The sun became veiled by the clouds; it began to rain. The jaguar swam a little more, but then exited the water. It walked back to the jungle for twenty minutes in the rain. When the jaguar arrived on its turf, it climbed up a tree and fell asleep. The moon looked like a summer mango.

The Tattoo of Moctezuma

A man got a tattoo of Moctezuma, the last fully independent ruler of the Aztec Empire. In the tattoo artwork, Moctezuma has on an elaborate headdress with golden covering and iridescent green quetzal feathers. He also has a shield in the tattoo for a battle he can't win. Moctezuma has a lengthy, strong spear. The skin of Moctezuma is dark brown like the man's skin color. The man gets the tattoo on his forearm, to show strength. On the other forearm, he has a tattoo of Hernán Cortés with a sword, to show symmetry.

Thank You

I would like to thank my family for their continued support. My parents are one of the main reasons I became a writer. Thank you. Thank you to my siblings, brothers-in-law, nieces, nephews, tíos and tías.

Thank you to my childhood/adolescent group of friends: Anthony Chavez, Jon Adame, Mike Perez (R.I.P.), Brandon Singh, Andy Velasquez, Carlos Luevano, Jason Chua, Rey Lechuga, Clyde Aaron, and anyone I forgot. Thanks for the memories.

Thank you to the editors of Sundress Publications for working with me on this manuscript; I appreciate the support and care.

Thank you to my elementary school teachers, high school teachers, high school football coaches, college professors.

Thank you to my students, anyone who has ever taken a workshop or class with me. Thank you.

Thank you to poets who inspire me: Eduardo C. Corral, Steve Castro, Kimberly Southwick, Rodney Gomez, Dr. M. Cynthia Cheung, Lena Zycinsky, Puneet Dutt, Amanda Chiado, Zach Powers, Jennifer Maritza McCauley, Michael Torres, Allison Hedge Coke, Virgil Suarez, Felicia Zamora, Francisco X. Alarcon (R.I.P.), James Tate (R.I.P.), Dean Young (R.I.P.), Charles Simic (R.I.P.), Alberto Rios, Ada Limon.

Thank you to the National Endowment for the Arts Fellowship, the Carolyn Moore Writers House and Portland Community College, the University of California at Riverside, and the University of Tennessee at Knoxville.

Lastly, thank you, truly, to the readers of poetry and poets everywhere.

About the Author

Jose Hernandez Diaz is a 2017 NEA Poetry Fellow. He is the author of a chapbook of prose poems: *The Fire Eater* (Texas Review Press, 2020) and *Bad Mexican, Bad American* (Acre Books, 2024). His work appears in *The American Poetry Review, Boulevard, Cincinnati Review, The Common, Huizache, Iowa Review, The Missouri Review, Poetry, Sixth Finch, The Southern Review, Yale Review*, and in *The Best American Nonrequired Reading*. He teaches generative workshops for Hugo House, Lighthouse Writers Workshops, The Writer's Center, Beyond Baroque, and elsewhere. He serves as a Poetry Mentor in The Adroit Journal Summer Mentorship Program.

Other Sundress Titles

Florence
Bess Cooley
16.99

Spoke the Dark Matter
Michelle Whittaker
$12.99

Back to Alabama
Valerie A. Smith
$12.99

DANGEROUS BODIES/
ANGER ODES
stevie redwood
$12.99

Slaughterhouse for Old Wives' Tales
Hannah V Warren
$12.99

Good Son
Kyle Liang
$12.99

Grief Slut
Evelyn Berry
$12.99

Nocturne in Joy
Tatiana Johnson-Boria
$12.99

Ruin & Want
José Angel Araguz
$17.99

Another Word for Hunger
Heather Bartlett
$12.99

Age of Forgiveness
Caleb Curtiss
$12.99

Little Houses
Athena Nassar
$12.99

www.ingramcontent.com/pod-product-compliance
Lightning Source LLC
Chambersburg PA
CBHW031144090426
42738CB00008B/1219